Dinosaur Families

Unearth the secrets behind dinosaur fossils

QEB Publishing

Rupert Matthews

DINOSAUR DIG

Copyright © QEB Publishing 2008

First published in the USA in 2008 by QEB Publishing Inc
23062 La Cadena Drive
Laguna Hills, CA 92653

www.qeb-publishing.com

Library of Congress Control Number: 2008011535

ISBN 978 1 59566 548 5

Printed and bound in China

Author Rupert Matthews
Consultant Neil Clark
Editor Amanda Askew
Designer Liz Wiffen

Publisher Steve Evans
Creative Director Zeta Davies

Picture credits (t = top, b = bottom, l = left, r = right)
Alamy Kim Karpeles 24
Corbis Louie Psihoyos 4, Louie Psihoyos 7, Louie Psihoyos 11, DK Limited 15, Louie Psihoyo 17, Dung Vo Trung 18, Kevin Schafer 21
Shutterstock Michael C Gray 2
Topfoto ImageWork 8

Words in **bold** can be found in the glossary on page 31.

CONTENTS

DINO GUIDE

For every dinosaur in this book and many more, learn how to pronounce their name, find out their length and weight, and discover what they ate.

DINOSAUR DIG

Dinosaurs **were** reptiles **that lived on Earth. They became** extinct **about 65 million years ago. There are no dinosaurs alive today.**

Scientists called **paleontologists** (pay-lee-on-toll-oh-jists) study dinosaurs. By examining dinosaur remains, called **fossils**, paleontologists can show what dinosaurs looked like when they were alive.

◗ *Paleontologist Jack Horner has excavated, or dug up, a nest of fossilized dinosaur eggs in the USA.*

1 A dinosaur dies on a lakeshore

3 The **skeleton** sinks into the lake

Many dinosaur remains have been found—of **adults**, youngsters, babies, and even of eggs in nests. These remains help paleontologists to understand how dinosaur families lived and behaved.

How big were dinosaurs?

Every dinosaur is compared to an average adult, about 5 feet 2 in height, to show just how big they really were.

⬤ *When a plant or animal dies, it usually rots away completely. However, in special conditions, parts of it can become fossilized.*

4

5

Layers of mud settle over the skeleton. The mud and bones gradually turn into stone

The rock wears away, or **erodes**

As more rock erodes, the skeleton is revealed

CARING FOR THE EGGS

Dinosaurs laid eggs, which were kept warm and safe until they hatched into babies.

In hot areas, the eggs were laid on the warm ground. The mother dinosaur would stay nearby to provide shade from the sun if the eggs became too hot.

In cooler parts of the world, the mother dinosaur may have piled leaves on top of the eggs. As the leaves rotted, they produced heat, which kept the eggs warm.

DINOSAUR DIG
Jobaria

WHERE: Niger, Africa

PERIOD: 110 million years ago in the early Cretaceous

DIG SITE

WOW!

In July 1923, Roy Chapman Andrews and his team found the first dinosaur eggs in Mongolia, Asia— they were *Oviraptor* (oh-vee-rap-tor) eggs.

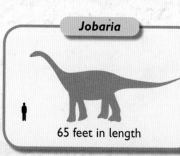

Jobaria

65 feet in length

◐ This model shows a baby dinosaur inside its egg. The baby feeds on the sac, or bag, of orange yolk. It breathes the oxygen that filters through the egg shell.

◐ A mother Jobaria (joe-barr-ee-ah) tries to drive off a smaller hunting dinosaur. Many dinosaur eggs were eaten before they had a chance to hatch.

THE NURSERY

Some dinosaurs built large nurseries **where more than 100 dinosaurs laid their eggs in nests close to each other.**

After the eggs hatched, the adult dinosaurs brought food to their young and guarded the nursery from attack. The babies stayed in the nest for several weeks.

Hunting dinosaurs may have cared for their babies in a similar way. Young hunters probably followed their parents for several months so that they could learn how to hunt successfully.

DIG SITE

◗ Maiasaura *(my-yah-saw-rah)* *would hatch from their eggs* *after eight to ten weeks.*

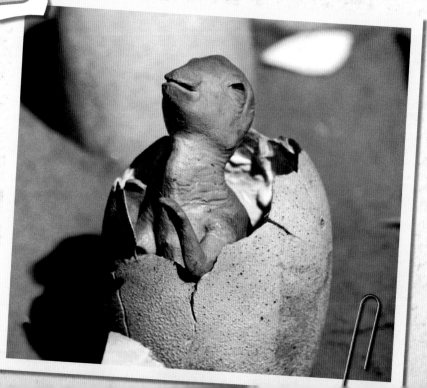

The young Maiasaura stayed in the nursery for several weeks after they hatched, so they could be cared for by their parents.

Maiasaura

30 feet in length

YOUNGSTERS

Young animals, including dinosaurs, look and behave differently from adults.

Their head and eyes are large in proportion to their body—this makes their body look too small! Their legs tend to be shorter and thicker than those of adults.

Mussaurus (muss-saw-rus) had a large head, large eyes, and short legs. Scientists think that the fossil they have found is of a baby animal. The adult would have been much larger and looked different.

DINOSAUR DIG
Mussaurus

WHERE: Argentina, South America

PERIOD: 215 million years ago in the late Triassic

DIG SITE

◗ *A baby* Mussaurus *would only have been 8 inches in length—about the size of a rat.*

WOW!

Fossils of a young *Tyrannosaurus* (tie-rann-oh-saw-rus) have been found. The remains show that it was probably a fierce killer, just like the adult.

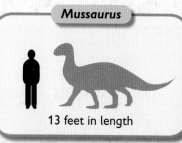

Mussaurus

13 feet in length

⬤ The fossil of Mussaurus is one of the smallest dinosaur skeletons ever found, but it is of a baby. The adult would have been about 13 feet in length.

LEAVING THE NEST

Not all dinosaurs cared for their young in nurseries. Some youngsters had to look after themselves.

Young **sauropods**, such as *Apatosaurus* (ap-at-oh-saw-rus), hid from hunters in bushes and other **undergrowth**. As they grew larger, the youngsters may have left the safety of cover as they were able to fight off attackers.

Fossil footprints show that sauropods waded into lakes or rivers. They may have been hiding or escaping from hunters.

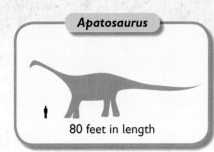

Apatosaurus

80 feet in length

Young sauropods, such as Apatosaurus, left the nest when they were only a few days old. Adults collected soft plants for the babies to eat when they hatched, but then they ignored their young.

Some scientists believe that baby dinosaurs sometimes followed their parents instead of living by themselves.

A young dinosaur relied on its parent for protection against attack. The youngster would have learned many skills by watching its parent, including which plants were good to eat, which food to avoid, and which dinosaurs were dangerous hunters.

DINOSAUR DIG
Cetiosaurus

WHERE: England, Europe

PERIOD: 180 million years ago in the mid Jurassic

DIG SITE

WOW!

In 1868, a complete Cetiosaurus skeleton was discovered by English paleontologist, Sir Richard Owen.

◗ The backbone of Cetiosaurus (set-ee-oh-saw-rus) looks similar to a whale's, which is why the creature was given a name that means "whale lizard." At first, scientists thought Cetiosaurus was a sea animal, until fossils of the leg bones were found.

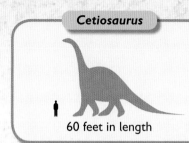

Cetiosaurus

60 feet in length

◗ *A young Cetiosaurus follows its parent across open ground. The adult would protect its young as well as teaching it how to survive.*

UNDER ATTACK

Some dinosaurs lived together in groups called herds. The fully grown adults would join together to protect the youngsters.

Herds of animals work together. If a hunter, such as *Tyrannosaurus* (tie-rann-oh-saw-rus), threatened to attack a herd of *Triceratops* (try-ser-ah-tops), they would form a circle.

The adults stood on the outside of the circle with their sharp horns facing outward to protect the youngsters standing on the inside. *Tyrannosaurus* would be unable to reach the young, so it would give up the hunt and leave.

DINOSAUR DIG
Triceratops ....
.... Tyrannosaurus

WHERE: Colorado, North America ....
PERIOD: 65 million years ago in the late Cretaceous ....

DIG SITE

WOW!

Scientists have found 20 *Tyrannosaurus* skeletons—more than of any other large hunting dinosaur.

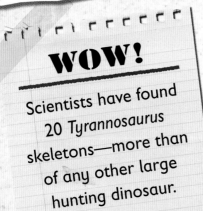

◐ *Tyrannosaurus cannot break into a circle of defending Triceratops. However, it may return later to try to grab a youngster by surprise.*

Tyrannosaurus

40 feet in length

A complete fossilized skeleton of Triceratops. Its large horns may have been used to fight other dinosaurs, including hunters.

Triceratops

30 feet in length

GOING IT ALONE

As a young dinosaur grew older, it would become stronger and begin to learn the skills it needed to survive.

Eventually a youngster would be able to look after itself. Instead of following its parent everywhere, the youngster may gradually start to drift away and begin to live on its own.

Iguanodon (ig-wan-oh-don) fed on shrubs and small trees. A young *Iguanodon* may stay with its parent for a year or two before it left to live by itself.

DINOSAUR DIG
Iguanodon

WHERE: England, Europe

WHEN: 140 million years ago in the early Cretaceous

DIG SITE

◗ *An adult* Iguanodon *jawbone. A youngster would have had a similar jaw and teeth as it ate the same food.*

Iguanodon

33 feet in length

◗ *A young Iguanodon tries to keep up with its parent. The adult dinosaur would gradually lose interest in its young as it grew older. Eventually they would separate.*

THREAT DISPLAYS

Adults may have been forced to compete with other dinosaurs of the same type.

If there was little food, survival depended on finding good feeding grounds. It is thought that some hunters may have had a home area, or territory, where they would not allow others of their kind to hunt.

DINOSAUR DIG
Dilophosaurus

WHERE: Arizona, North America

WHEN: 190 million years ago in the early Jurassic

DIG SITE

WOW!

The bones in the crests of Dilophosaurus were as thin as paper in places.

Dilophosaurus (die-low-fo-saw-rus) had a pair of bony **crests** growing from the top of its **skull**. Scientists believe that the dinosaur may have used these crests in a threat display to scare away hunters.

◑ This fossil of Dilophosaurus is almost complete, although some of the bones have become mixed up. The crests on its head can clearly be seen.

◑ A pair of rival Dilophosaurus display their crests to each other by pacing back and forth. A fight would only take place if neither dinosaur backed down.

Dilophosaurus

20 feet in length

POWER STRUGGLE

Sometimes threats and displays would not settle a struggle between dinosaurs. They would often fight to decide which was the strongest.

Stegoceras (steg-oh-sair-ass) was a **bonehead** dinosaur. It had a very thick skull with a dome of solid bone on top of its head. Some scientists think that *Stegoceras* fought each other using their heads.

🔘 Stegoceras *fought by charging toward each other. The force used when they crashed together would soon show which dinosaur was the strongest.*

DIG SITE

WOW!

Stegoceras skulls could be as much as 3 inches in thickness. Males had thicker skulls than females.

Stegoceras would run at each other with their heads lowered. They would crash together with enormous force. After a few impacts, the weaker dinosaur would give up the fight. Scientists believe that they probably hit each other on the sides of the body, rather than head-butting.

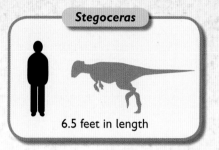

Stegoceras

6.5 feet in length

HERD INSTINCT

Some sauropods, such as *Mamenchisaurus* (ma-men-key-saw-rus), lived in herds—from as few as ten dinosaurs to as many as 100.

Living in a herd had advantages because one or two dinosaurs would always be looking out for danger. The dinosaurs could join forces to drive off a hunter. In a herd, plant eaters could find water or good eating grounds more easily.

◗ *Mamenchisaurus may have been able to rear up on its back legs, using the tail to balance. Then Mamenchisaurus could feed on even higher leaves on trees.*

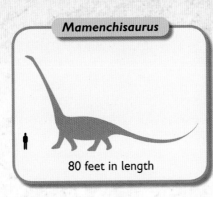

Mamenchisaurus

80 feet in length

WOW!

Mamenchisaurus had the longest neck of any dinosaur. It was more than 30 feet in length—that's the same as six people lying end to end.

⬤ A herd of sauropods wanders across a dry plain. Fossil footprints show that younger animals stayed in the center of the herd where they would be protected from attack.

All dinosaurs eventually died. Some were killed by hunters or died after a fight. Others fell victim to disease or to an accident. Some probably just died of old age.

DINOSAUR DIG
Leaellynasaura
WHERE: Victoria, Australia

WHEN: 110 million years ago in the mid Cretaceous

DIG SITE

Leaellynasaura (lee-ell-in-ah-saw-rah) lived in Australia. Millions of years ago, the winters would have been very cold. If *Leaellynasaura* could not keep warm enough, it may have died from the cold.

When a dinosaur died, its body was most likely either to be eaten by the first hunter to find it or to rot away completely. The bones or teeth of only a few creatures remained as fossils.

A dinosaur that died next to a river had a better chance of being fossilized as its body would have been quickly covered by mud or sand.

WOW!

A large number of bones has been found in Alberta, Canada. Scientists believe that hundreds of dinosaurs were swept away by a fast-flowing river.

A dead **Leaellynasaura** lies beside a frozen river. It is thought that the long, cold winters may have killed off many weaker dinosaurs.

Leaellynasaura

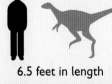

6.5 feet in length

DINO GUIDE

Coelophysis
PRONUNCIATION
see-low-fye-sis
LENGTH 10 feet
WEIGHT 75–80 pounds
DIET Small animals

Mussaurus (p10)
PRONUNCIATION
muss-saw-rus
LENGTH 13 feet (adult)
WEIGHT 330 pounds
DIET Plants

Efraasia
PRONUNCIATION
ef-rah-see-ah
LENGTH 23 feet
WEIGHT 1,300 pounds
DIET Plants

Pisanosaurus
PRONUNCIATION
peez-an-oh-saw-rus
LENGTH 3 feet
WEIGHT 6.5 pounds
DIET Plants

Eoraptor
PRONUNCIATION
ee-oh-rap-tor
LENGTH 3 feet
WEIGHT 7–30 pounds
DIET Small animals

Plateosaurus
PRONUNCIATION
plat-ee-oh-saw-rus
LENGTH 26 feet
WEIGHT 1 ton
DIET Plants

Herrerasaurus
PRONUNCIATION
he-ray-ra-saw-rus
LENGTH 10 feet
WEIGHT 450 pounds
DIET Animals

Riojasaurus
PRONUNCIATION
ree-oh-ha-saw-rus
LENGTH 33 feet
WEIGHT 1 ton
DIET Plants

Melanorosaurus
PRONUNCIATION
mel-an-or-oh-saw-rus
LENGTH 33 feet
WEIGHT 1 ton
DIET Plants

Staurikosaurus
PRONUNCIATION
store-ick-oh-saw-rus
LENGTH 6.5 feet
WEIGHT 65 pounds
DIET Small animals

Allosaurus
PRONUNCIATION
al-oh-saw-rus
LENGTH 40 feet
WEIGHT 1.5–2 tons
DIET Animals

Apatosaurus (p12)
PRONUNCIATION
ap-at-oh-saw-rus
LENGTH 80 feet
WEIGHT 25–35 tons
DIET Plants

Ceratosaurus
PRONUNCIATION
se-rat-oh-saw-rus
LENGTH 20 feet
WEIGHT 1,500–1,900 pounds
DIET Animals

Cetiosaurus (p14)
PRONUNCIATION
set-ee-oh-saw-rus
LENGTH 60 feet
WEIGHT 15–20 tons
DIET Plants

Dilophosaurus (p20)
PRONUNCIATION
die-low-fo-saw-rus
LENGTH 20 feet
WEIGHT 880 pounds
DIET Animals

Mamenchisaurus (p24)
PRONUNCIATION
ma-men-key-saw-rus
LENGTH 80 feet
WEIGHT 12–15 tons
DIET Plants

Megalosaurus
PRONUNCIATION
meg-ah-low-saw-rus
LENGTH 30 feet
WEIGHT 1 ton
DIET Plants

Ornitholestes
PRONUNCIATION
or-nith-oh-less-teez
LENGTH 6.5 feet
WEIGHT 65 pounds
DIET Animals

Sinosauropteryx
PRONUNCIATION
sy-no-saw-op-tur-iks
LENGTH 3 feet
WEIGHT 6.5 pounds
DIET Small animals

Stegosaurus
PRONUNCIATION
steg-oh-saw-rus
LENGTH 26–30 feet
WEIGHT 2–3 tons
DIET Plants

Euoplocephalus
PRONUNCIATION
you-oh-ploe-sef-ah-lus
LENGTH 20–23 feet
WEIGHT 2 tons
DIET Plants

Monoclonius
PRONUNCIATION
mon-oh-clone-ee-us
LENGTH 16.5 feet
WEIGHT 2–3 tons
DIET Plants

Iguanodon (p18)
PRONUNCIATION
ig-wan-oh-don
LENGTH 33 feet
WEIGHT 4–5 tons
DIET Plants

Oviraptor (p6)
PRONUNCIATION
oh-vee-rap-tor
LENGTH 6.5 feet
WEIGHT 65 pounds
DIET Small animals and plants

Jobaria (p6)
PRONUNCIATION
joe-barr-ee-ah
LENGTH 65 feet
WEIGHT 18–20 tons
DIET Plants

Stegoceras (p22)
PRONUNCIATION
steg-oh-sair-ass
LENGTH 6.5 feet
WEIGHT 110–150 pounds
DIET Plants

Leaellynasaura (p26)
PRONUNCIATION
lee-ell-in-ah-saw-rah
LENGTH 6.5 feet
WEIGHT 22 pounds
DIET Plants

Triceratops (p16)
PRONUNCIATION
try-ser-ah-tops
LENGTH 30 feet
WEIGHT 5–8 tons
DIET Plants

Maiasaura (p8)
PRONUNCIATION
my-yah-saw-rah
LENGTH 30 feet
WEIGHT 3–4 tons
DIET Plants

Tyrannosaurus (p16)
PRONUNCIATION
tie-rann-oh-saw-rus
LENGTH 40 feet
WEIGHT 6 tons
DIET Large animals

GLOSSARY

Adult An animal that is fully grown.

Bonehead A type of dinosaur that had a thick layer of bone on top of its skull.

Crest Bone on the top of the head.

Cretaceous The third period of time in the age of the dinosaurs. The Cretaceous began about 145 million years ago and ended about 65 million years ago.

Dinosaur A type of reptile that lived millions of years ago. All dinosaurs are now extinct.

Erode To wear away.

Extinct Not existing any more. An animal is extinct when they have all died out.

Fossil Any part of a plant or animal that has been preserved in rock. Also traces of plants or animals, such as footprints.

Hatch To emerge from an egg.

Herd A group of animals that lives together.

Jurassic The second period of time in the age of the dinosaurs. The Jurassic began about 206 million years ago and ended about 145 million years ago.

Nursery A place where dinosaurs went to hatch their babies and where the young lived for some time afterward.

Paleontologist A scientist who studies ancient forms of life, including dinosaurs.

Reptile A cold-blooded animal, such as a lizard. Dinosaurs were reptiles, too.

Sauropod A type of dinosaur that had a long neck and tail. Sauropods included the largest of all dinosaurs.

Skeleton The bones in an animal's body.

Skull The bones of the head of an animal. The skull does not include the jaw, but many skulls have jaws attached.

Triassic The first period of time in the age of the dinosaurs. The Triassic began about 248 million years ago and ended about 208 million years ago.

Undergrowth Bushes, small trees, and other plants that grow under bigger plants and trees.

INDEX